S0-CFN-394

PICTURE PICTURE
PERFECT PERFECT

URE PICTURE PICTUI
ECT PERFECT PERFE

PICTURE PICTURE
PERFECT PERFECT

URE PICTURE PICTUI
ECT PERFECT PERFE

DR. SHAPIRO'S

PICTURE
PERFECT
WEIGHT
LOSS

DR. SHAPIRO'S

PICTURE
PERFECT
WEIGHT
LOSS

Dr. Howard M. Shapiro

RUNNING PRESS
PHILADELPHIA • LONDON

A Running Press® Miniature Edition™

Text 2000 by Dr. Howard M. Shapiro

Photography © Kurt Wilson/Rodale Images and Lou Manna

Printed in China

Library of Congress Cataloging-in-Publication Number
00-135516

ISBN 0-7624-0982-7

This book may be ordered by mail from the publisher.
Please include $1.00 for postage and handling.
But try your bookstore first!

Running Press Book Publishers
125 South Twenty-second Street
Philadelphia, PA 19103-4399

Introduction

*F*ed up with diets?

You're not alone.

For nearly 20 years, I have specialized in weight control at my practice in mid-Manhattan.

I used to think New Yorkers were unique in their weight concerns. But of course they're not. Millions of people across America want to lose weight. And they're searching for the best way to do it.

Once you develop Food Awareness Training—using the techniques in this book—you'll never have to count calories or grams of fat. You don't have to avoid restaurants or dodge dinner invitations.

After Food Awareness Training, one look is all it takes to help you make your choices. Weight loss becomes automatic because you react automatically.

I don't tell my patients what they can't eat or shouldn't eat. Instead, I talk about the choices that they can make. I ask them to subscribe to a few principles that, I believe, are the essential components of successful weight loss.

Look– No Bad Foods

• **Any reason for eating is okay.** If you crave food, go right ahead and have some. Just eat the healthiest, lowest-calorie foods you find satisfying.

• **There are no bad foods.** There are times when only the high-fat, high calorie foods will do. You're not cheating if you eat them, but there are also many alternatives.

• **There are no correct portions.** Hunger varies from person to person. Even if you eat a whole pint of sorbet, your diet isn't a failure.

• **An eating plan needs to suit your tastes and lifestyle.** You can continue your normal activities without interruption as you continue to work toward losing weight.

• **You're never on a diet.** You're participating in an ongoing process of learning to make satisfying food choices.

Why Deprivation
Diets Don't Work

To lose weight successfully, you either have to decrease your caloric intake or increase the number of calories expended through exercise—preferably both. To lose weight successfully and keep it off, you have to accomplish calorie reduction without feeling deprived. Feeling deprived kicks you in the rear end—right in the direction of the nearest hot-fudge sundae or the local bakery.

In Command of Appetite

Deep in the command center of your brain, a newly discovered protein, GLP-1, is playing an important role in telling you when you're feeling full. When you eat, it tells the intestines and pancreas to slow down digestion.

In animal studies, rats injected with GLP-1 showed signs that they were full before they finished their normal rations of food. When an inhibitor of GLP-1 was injected, the rats ate more than usual and grew fatter.

People who are attempting to lose weight typically do not report feelings of deprivation; they bury them instead. They will say things like, "I had plenty. I didn't need to eat the brownie"; "I wasn't hungry."; or "I don't know why I did it."

If those phrases sound familiar, I can assure you that people who are deprived of food do need to eat. If you eat, it's because you're hungry.

Liquid Lunch

Today, the phrase "liquid lunch" refers to dieters using meals-in-a-can as a lunch replacement.

There's a problem, however. While most of the weight-loss "shakes" contain a number of vitamins and minerals, they also contain substantial numbers of calories and fat—in fact, they're identical to the calorie and fat content of an 8-ounce chocolate milkshake.

You're Choosing,
Not Cheating

With Food Awareness Training, you're always choosing, never cheating. So you never have to feel like you're falling off the wagon. And you never have to live up to impossible standards.

Obviously, you can't have every dessert in the world and still lose weight. But you do have some choices. You can pass up dessert, you can eat it, or you can choose one of many lower-calorie alternatives that may be just as satisfying. I recommend you substitute the lower-calorie foods when possible, but have the brownie or the roll every now and then.

Concealed Calories in "Reduced-Fat'

When you see the label "reduced-fat," you may think you've found something that can help you lose weight. But before you take the product to the check-out counter, check the calorie count. Manufacturers tend to compensate for the lower fat in many of these products by loading them with sugar and other carbohydrates.

Less Fat, Same Cals

Tufts University researchers compared some regular and reduced-fat products. The results explain why Americans who eat them still gain weight.

½ cup Campbell's Vegetable Soup (with beef stock)
= 80 calories

½ cup Campbell's 98% Fat-Free Healthy Request Vegetable Soup (with beef stock)
= 80 calories

2 Drake's Yodels
= 280 calories

2 Drake's reduced-fat Yodels
= 290 calories

2 Tbsp Jif peanut butter
= 190 calories

2 Tbsp reduced-fat Jif peanut
butter
= 190 calories

But please, whatever you do, recognize that the decision is up to you. Making a conscious decision to enjoy something is very different from eating it and feeling like a failure. In the latter case, people often go on to an all-out binge, having decided that it doesn't matter since they've already blown the diet.

What's a Lot and What's Not

Unfortunately, most veteran dieters expect the acceptable

foods to be something like lettuce leaves and celery stalks. We're suggesting food that you may decide to substitute for higher-calorie foods while getting the same satisfying taste.

Do you like chocolate ice cream? You can have the richest chocolate ice cream available— for about 1,350 calories a pint. But you have other choices. You can have chocolate frozen yogurt or sorbet—those have 450 calories a pint or less. If you think that a frozen fudge bar or two would be just as satisfying, you're really in luck, since a low-calorie fudge bar is only 30 calories. In other words, you'd have to eat 45 fudge bars to consume the same number of calories that you'd get from one pint of rich ice cream.

Dressing Down

Researchers report that salad dressing is a major source of fat in the American diet. Commercial dressings are primarily fat, with 85 percent of their calories from oil. Instead, try the fat-free or low-fat commercial dressings or make your own lower-fat vinegar-and-oil dressing, stretching it with lemon or tomato juice and a range of condiments such as ketchup, salsa, relish, and hot sauce.

Calories and Where They Come From

As you're making food choices, you will naturally lean towards foods that have lower calorie counts, since it's reasonable to assume that you want to lose weight. But in addition to this, I'd like to steer you toward foods that are high in nutritional value. And, of course, it's a good way to make sure you're getting all the vitamins, minerals, fiber, and protein that your body needs.

In Praise of Beans

Beans offer the person trying to lose weight a double dose of benefits. First, they are low in fat and packed with nutrients: fiber, phytochemicals, folate, protein, magnesium, potassium, zinc, copper, iron, and vitamins. Second, the potential they offer for culinary creativity is as staggering as their variety.

Nutrients are divided into two basic categories, macronutrients and micronutrients. Macronutrients are food substances like protein, fat, and carbohydrates that end up supplying us with calories.

A macronutrient has the potential to supply energy, and the actual production of energy is measured in calories. Calories are calculated by measuring the amount of heat a food gives off when it is "burned."

Micronutrients are food components like vitamins and minerals. These supply no calories, but they help release energy from food.

Try This Substitution

Instead of one 6-ounce hamburger, try two 3-ounce veggie burgers. What you give up are fat and cholesterol—about 20 grams of the former and 150 milligrams of the latter. What you gain is fiber and the other nutrients contained in the soy that make up the veggie burgers.

What's in a Lite Suds?

What's light in "lite" beers is the calorie count. To be considered light, a beer must have at least 25 percent fewer calories than regular beer. Most brands of light beer have about 100 calories in 12 ounces, versus regular beer with anywhere from 140 to 200 calories per 12 ounces.

What about water? Technically, it doesn't fit in either category. It's not a macronutrient, because it has no calories. And it's not a micronutrient, because it's neither a vitamin nor a mineral.

But we all need water to live. It's absolutely essential for digestion as well as many other bodily processes.

Fluid Facts

Drink when you're thirsty. Thirst is a fairly reliable indicator of the need for fluids.

Don't scorn soda. The fluid in soda does count, especially if you're drinking a low-sodium low-carbohydrate beverage such as a diet drink.

Count tea and coffee, too. Though caffeine is a mild diuretic, when you drink a caffeinated beverage, your body still retains as much as half the fluid.

Shopping Low-Calorie

By reading the Nutrition Facts label carefully, you can quickly learn how much of certain good-guy nutrients like vitamins A and C, calcium, iron, and fiber the food contains. Compare those figures with the percentage Daily Value for such "bad guys" as saturated fat and cholesterol. If the label reveals that you're getting just 2 to 3 percent of the good guys while you're getting 20 to 30 percent of the bad guys, you know immediately you're on the wrong side of the tracks.

Label Lingo Lesson

Food-label terms have some strict definitions, but you won't find those definitions on most labels.

• A low-fat food has 3 grams or less of fat.

• Foods with low saturated fat contain 1 gram or less of saturated fat.

• A low-sodium food has 140 milligrams or less of sodium.

• "Very low sodium" means 35 milligrams or less of sodium per serving.

- Low-cholesterol means 20 milligrams or less of cholesterol and also 2 grams or less of saturated fat.
- Low-calorie foods have 40 calories or less per serving.
- Lean meat or poultry must contain less than 10 grams of fat, 4.5 grams or less of saturated fat, and less than 95 milligrams of cholesterol per serving.
- An extra-lean serving has less than 5 grams of fat, less than 2 grams of saturated fat, and less than 95 milligrams of cholesterol.

The Exercise Component

Every health professional in the country advises patients that exercise is important. Exercise helps prevent disease by strengthening your immune system. It makes you feel better, sleep better, work better. It improves your appearance. It raises your energy level. It even lifts your mood. And, proven beyond all doubt, exercise helps you lose and control weight.

Flexing through the Next Traffic Jam

Cut the stress out of your road trip and burn calories too! Try these exercises:

- Press your lower back into the seat and tighten your abdomen muscles for a few seconds.
- Lift both shoulders. Hold. Then release.
- Move your head forward and from side to side.
- Tighten every muscle in your body. Relax.

Research increasingly confirms that even short bouts of exercise, spaced intermittently throughout the day, enhance your overall fitness and contribute to weight control. A brisk walk up and down stairs, 10 minutes of lifting homemade weights, a quarter of an hour on the stationary bike all provide boosts to your system. And, say researchers, what counts is the total accumulation of exercise in a 24-hour period. In other words, whenever you exercise, it's beneficial.

Monitoring the Monitor

If you're accustomed to watching yourself burn calories—literally—on the monitor on your exercise machine, be aware that the reading you get is not really a precise count, even if you've entered your age and weight.

What the machine monitor can provide, however, is a relative assessment of calorie-burning. In other words, if you continue to use the same machine, you'll be able to see your improvement over time.

The Write Stuff:
Your Own Food Diary

Now that you know that it's about making choices, it's time to begin keeping a food diary to see the choices you make. As you build awareness of your food habits and begin to see patterns in your eating, you will also begin to take more responsibility for your food choices.

Above all, you'll learn to be in touch with how you feel about food and about your eating habits. By forcing you to pay attention to the feelings you have about food and eating, the food diary makes you aware of your own ability to make choices. That's why it's your first step toward better choices—choices that will help you lose weight and keep it off through your lifetime.

How to Start:

Make 7 copies of the template you find on page 45. For a week, record every bite and sip you take—with the exception of water and low-calorie beverages.

Write down what you've had the minute you've eaten it—immediately. If you put off making the notation, you will almost certainly omit an important item in your entry.

Here's how to fill out each entry on the diary template.

• **Time.** Record the exact time that you are eating. Does the diary show that at certain times of the day you tend to eat more? Are other food choices available to you at those times?

• **Food.** Note what you have eaten, and how it was prepared, if applicable. Describe as many ingredients in the dish as you think necessary. What kind of choices do you make? Are you choosing mostly protein? Mostly starch? Or was it starch in the morning and protein in the afternoon?

• **Degree of Hunger.** For the purpose of this diary, define hunger as a desire to eat regardless of reason. Rate the desire on a scale from 0 to 4, with 0 indicating no hunger and 4 indicating extreme hunger. Does the diary show that you ate when you didn't feel truly hungry? Sometimes? Often?

• **Situation (Place/Activity).** Where, and in what situation, were you when you had the food or drink? This information is helpful because I don't want you to change your lifestyle, just your relationship with food. Can you find any connection between the situation in which you found yourself and the fact that you reached for food? You may be able to see the connection between the situation and the kind of food you chose.

• **Comments.** Note anything you feel is relevant to your food choice or to the way you felt after eating. What do your comments tell you about your eating habits?

After you have scrupulously kept your food diary for a week sit down, look it over, and get ready to evaluate it.

You're looking for patterns—recurring situations in which you make food choices. The diary helps you see where you've chosen a high-calorie option or the less-healthful alternative.

Be honest and candid as you evaluate your food diary. Remember: This is an exercise in awareness. Nobody is asking you—now or ever—to change your eating habits or patterns in terms of when, why, or how you eat. The aim will be to find healthier, lower-calorie ways of working with those patterns. To get there, you must start with awareness.

The Food Diary

Time	Food (Preparation, Serving Size)	Degree of Hunger (0-4)	Situation (Place, Activity)	Comments

Fiber Feasts

Want to add fiber without any calorie penalty? The comparisons listed here show how you can fill up on fiber—and get lots of additional nutrients—without adding a single calorie.

1½ cups chicken noodle soup
150 calories
No fiber

1½ cups minestrone soup
110 calories
10 grams of fiber

3 oz turkey on Italian bread
290 calories
No fiber

VS.

3 oz veggie lunchmeat
on 5-grain bread with
lettuce, tomato,
and coleslaw
240 calories
6 grams of fiber

Elegant Eats

Want to start your meal with a touch of class?

An ounce of liver pâté has 130 calories without the bread or toast points or crackers to spread it on. Or you can have 3 oz. of smoked salmon, touched up with the pungent flavor of capers and the cool taste of cucumber.

Equal Calories, Different Portions

1 oz liver pâté
130 calories

=

3 oz smoked salmon with capers
and cucumber 130 calories

Equal Calories, Different Portions

No More Waffling
on Bagels

Naked and unadorned, a half a bagel has just 200 calories—the same calorie count as the light waffle breakfast pictured here.

½ dry bagel (2 ½ oz) 200 calories

Equal Calories, Different Portions

2 light waffles 140 calories
2 Tbsp light syrup 50 calories
berries 10 calories

TOTAL 200 calories

More for Less

A Whole New Burger Ball Game

Here's how an all-vegetable Boca burger—with a whole lot of fixings—compares to the classic American hamburger. Check it out:

1 hamburger (6 oz) 480 calories

bun 110 calories

fixings 10 calories

TOTAL 600 calories

VS.

More for Less

1 Boca burger (vegetarian) 85 calories
bun 110 calories
fixings 10 calories
2 portobello mushrooms 30 calories
2 slices eggplant 20 calories

TOTAL 255 calories

Sausage or Dill?

Consider that 32 large dill pickles have the same number of calories as one small sausage (1¾ oz.). Think about skipping the sausage and picking the pickles. They offer the salty taste you want—but without the saturated fats, cholesterol, and calories of sausage.

1 sausage (1¾ oz) 160 calories

Equal Calories, Different Portions

32 large dill pickles
160 calories

Roll It

Even without the butter and/or jam you love to spread on top or inside, this croissant costs 320 calories. Now picture what you can have instead, if you happen to be hungry for a lot of bread-stuff—both the bialy and the kaiser roll.

1 croissant (3 oz) 320 calories

Equal Calories, Different Portions

1 bialy **140** calories
1 kaiser roll **180** calories

TOTAL 320 calories

Hot Dog!

If you try the platter of three veggie hot dogs, you'll get the equivalent number of calories that you find in the chicken frank. And since the veggie dogs' protein is from a vegetable rather than an animal source, they're also far healthier.

Equal Calories, Different Portions

1 chicken frank 120 calories

3 veggie hot dogs 120 calories

Trade Deficit

A bagel is low-cal if I don't put any spread on it, you think to yourself. And it's filling, too. But contrast a bite of bagel with this vegetarian ham sandwich—a healthy entire meal. Next time you reach for a bagel, consider whether that's what you really want.

⅓ dry bagel (1½ oz) 140 **calories**

Equal Calories, Different Portions

vegetarian ham sandwich on light bread
with lettuce, tomato, mustard, and pickle
140 calories

Equal Calories, Different Portions

Phony "Baloney"/
Real Soy

The solo sandwich—naked bologna on naked pumpernickel—makes a 520-calorie lunch or snack. With the vegetable bologna option, you can also add soup and dessert to equal the same amount of calories!

4 oz bologna 360 calories

2 slices pumpernickel 160 calories

TOTAL 520 calories

Equal Calories, Different Portions

4 oz vegetable bologna 120 calories
2 slices pumpernickel 160 calories
1½ cups tomato vegetable soup 90 calories
3 cups mixed fruit 150 calories

TOTAL 520 calories

Eat the Starch, Hold the Fat

There's so much fat in these fries that you'll probably consume more calories from the frying fat than from the potato.

How about four ears of fresh corn instead? The calories are equivalent. Plus, eating corn is a lot more fun.

Equal Calories, Different Portions

1 medium serving french fries 360 calories

4 ears of corn on the cob 360 calories

Equal Calories, Different Portions

Lunch Package

The number of calories in that whole platter of five sandwiches made with low-calorie cheese is equivalent to the calories in a single croissant sandwich. With lettuce, tomato, and salsa on top of the cheese, these sandwiches are an excellent snack or lunch.

1 croissant with 3 oz cheese
650 calories

Equal Calories, Different Portions

1½ slices fat-free cheese
or soy substitute 40 calories
2 slices light wheat bread 80 calories
lettuce, tomato, and salsa 10 calories

TOTAL 130 calories

x 5 sandwiches TOTAL 650 calories

Equal Calories, Different Portions

A Little White Lie

The next time you reach for white rice, think of the other white choice that's shown here. Consider that 1 cup of almost zero nutrition rice has 220 calories—the same as these 10 cups of high-nutrition cauliflower.

1 cup white rice 220 calories

Equal Calories, Different Portions

10 cups cauliflower seasoned with herbs and grated Parmesan cheese
220 calories

Juice or Fruit

The calories in one glass of orange juice are equal to what you get from a whole pitcher of no-calorie orange beverage plus six oranges! The lesson? Don't waste calories on beverage consumption.

Equal Calories, Different Portions

1 glass (12 fl oz)
unsweetened orange juice
160 calories

=

1 pitcher diet orange
beverage O calories
6 small oranges
160 calories

Dig In . . .

Either the vegetable pepperoni or the shrimp has the caloric equivalent of one minute portion of regular meat pepperoni. There's even more to be said for the vegetable pepperoni and shrimp; both add nutrition benefits that you don't get from regular pepperoni.

Equal Calories, Different Portions

1 oz pepperoni 110 calories

**4 oz shrimp
110 calories**

4 oz vegetable pepperoni 110 calories

Bites and Bowls

This single bite of food is the caloric equivalent of the bowl of soup next to it. Honest. And in this case, the bowl of soup offers a treasury of nutrition.

Equal Calories, Different Portions

**1 chicken nugget (1 oz)
80 calories**

=

**1¼ cups vegetable
lentil soup 80 calories**

Well-Fed

At 700 calories, the single scone you see here is the caloric equivalent of an English muffin spread with jam, a dish of cherries, a bowl of corn flakes with banana, two slices of light toast with marmalade, the stem dish filled with sliced fruit, and a bowl of oatmeal with sliced peaches.

1 scone (7¾ oz) 700 calories

Equal Calories, Different Portions

1½ oz (dry weight) oatmeal with peaches 170 calories
English muffin with jam 150 calories
cherries 80 calories
corn flakes with banana 160 calories
2 slices light toast with marmalade 100 calories
orange and pineapple 40 calories

TOTAL 700 calories

Equal Calories, Different Portions

Starch Binge

The single square of corn bread with butter goes for 820 calories. You can have two ears of corn, a roll with jam, a baked potato topped with salsa, a sweet potato, and two slices of raisin bread for the same number of calories.

1 square of corn bread (7 oz)	700 calories
1 Tbsp butter	120 calories
TOTAL	**820 calories**

Equal Calories, Different Portions

2 ears of corn on the cob **170** calories
roll with jam **200** calories
baked potato with salsa **150** calories
sweet potato **160** calories
2 slices raisin bread **140** calories

TOTAL 820 calories

Bowled Over

Sure, these bowls look like they hold the same amount of cereal. But in terms of calories, the Grape-Nuts are about four times as calorie-laden. A bowl of Grape-Nuts costs 600 calories, compared to Cheerios' 165!

Equal Portions, Different Calories

1½ cups of Grape-Nuts
600 calories

VS.

1½ cups of Cheerios 165 calories

Four Cups

All of these salads are widely
available, but look at the differ-
ences in their calorie counts!

coleslaw (1 cup)
150 calories

potato salad (1 cup)
300 calories

Equal Portions, Different Calories

egg salad (1 cup)
640 calories

three-bean salad (1 cup)
180 calories

Skewed Skewers

A traditional skewer of lamb kabobs weighs in at 560 calories. But here's a tempting trade-off you're not likely to forget. For about one-fourth the calories, you can skewer the same amount of food in the form of scallops and mushrooms marinated in black bean sauce.

Equal Portions, Different Calories

8 oz lamb kabobs
560 calories

VS.

4 oz scallops **120** calories
4 oz mushrooms **15** calories
black bean sauce **15** calories

***

TOTAL **150** calories

Playing the Pizza Wheel

Traditional cheese pizza, not to mention cheese and pepperoni, hold no surprises: They're high in calories. Vegetable pizza, on the other hand, is a calorie bargain, as is a slice with tomato sauce and vegetable pepperoni. Add the nutritional power of these two pizza slices, and the bargain gets even better.

Equal Portions, Different Calories

cheese pizza
450 calories

veggie pepperoni pizza
250 calories

cheese and
pepperoni pizza
650 calories

vegetable pizza,
no cheese
250 calories

More for Less

Parlay Pizza

A couple slices of pizza? Instead of two slices, you might prefer just one slice of pizza along with a bowl of minestrone soup and a big serving of salad. In short, you'll get fewer calories from a three-course meal with nearly a full day's supply of vitamins, minerals, and fiber.

2 slices cheese pizza 900 calories

VS.

More for Less

1½ cups minestrone 110 calories
1 slice cheese pizza 450 calories
salad with artichoke hearts and tomatoes 40 calories

TOTAL 600 calories

More for Less

Not Enough Food on Your Plate

Who could feel deprived eating the platter on the right side, with its range of well-seasoned vegetables and its plentiful helping of tomato sauce?

3 cups pasta and tomato sauce **600** calories
zucchini **30** calories

TOTAL 630 calories

VS.

More for Less

1 cup pasta and tomato sauce 200 calories
1½ cups zucchini and eggplant 60 calories
acorn squash and mixed bell peppers 60 calories
portobello mushroom 20 calories
additional tomato sauce for vegetables 30 calories

TOTAL 370 calories

Looks are Deceptive

There's no calorie difference between the two dishes because the oil in the vinaigrette dressing brings the calorie count up to the level of the cream sauce.

Saboteurs

**3 cups pasta with
¼ cup creamy sauce
920 calories**

**3 cups spinach-and-tomato pasta
with ¼ cup vinaigrette dressing
920 calories**

Picture This:
The Weight is Over

Of course, I am not promising you that you will add years to your life, or that a funny and fabulous new personality will emerge. And I can't promise that you will become thinner than you've *ever* been when you change your relationship with food. What I am promising is that a changed relationship with food will add benefits to your life even as it subtracts pounds and takes away your fear of gaining weight.

Knowledge is power, as the saying goes, and the knowledge you gain from this book can give you the power you need to change the most constant, necessary, and ongoing relationship that you have—your relationship with food.

This book has been bound
using handcraft methods, and
Smyth-sewn to ensure durability.
The dust jacket was designed by
Christina Gaugler
and the interior was designed by
Terry Peterson.
The text was edited by
Victoria Hyun.
The text was set in Bembo,
Trade Gothic, and Bodoni.